About My Paintings
During a Soulful Mission

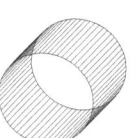

TOM OMIDI, Ph.D.
(also BA, MBA, MSMS, CGA,
and a former member of The Federation of Canadian Artists)

Copyright © 2022, 2025 by Tom Omidi

All rights reserved. No part of this book may be reproduced, translated, or transmitted in any form or by any means—graphic, electronic or mechanical, including photocopying, recording, taping or information storage or retrieval systems—without the prior written permission of the publisher or author.

Omidi, Tom, 1945-, author
About My Paintings
During a Soulful Mission
/ Tom Omidi, Ph.D.

ISBN 978-1-988351-17-9 (Paperback).
A copy of this book is held at
Library and Archives Canada Cataloguing in Publication

1. A Collection of Tom's Paintings (1996-2006).
2. The Background and Related Stories.
3. Philosophical Notions and Forces behind Painting
I. Title.

Front Cover: A View of Howe Sound: A Painting by Tom
Back Cover: Self-portrait by Tom

Published by Eros Books,
Vancouver, Canada

erosbooks2020@gmail.com

Printed in 2025

Author's Books
(As at 2025)[*]

Non-fictions (Sociology/Exploratory)   ISBN

The Nature of Love and Relationships   2011, 2016, **2020**   978-1-988351-03-2
Doubts and Decisions for Living:
    Volume I: The Foundation of Human Thoughts 2014, **2020**   978-1-988351-11-7
    Volume II: The Sanctity of Human Spirit   2014, **2020**   978-1-988351-12-4
    Volume III: The Structure of Human Life   2014, **2020**   978-1-988351-13-1
Relationship Facts, Trends, and Choices   2016, **2020**   978-1-988351-04-9
The Mysteries of Life, Love, and Happiness 2016, **2020**   978-1-988351-05-6
Marriage and Divorce Hardships   2016, **2020**   978-1-988351-06-3
Gender Qualities, Quirks, and Quarrels   2016, **2020**   978-1-988351-07-0
Relationship Needs, Framework, and Models 2016, **2020**   978-1-988351-08-7
Being Better Beings[1]   **2020**   978-1-988351-02-5
Humans versus Humanity[2]   **2025**   978-1-988351-19-3

Novels (Amusing/Autobiography)   ISBN

Persian Moons   2007, 2016, **2020**   978-1-988351-14-8
Midnight Gate-opener   2011, 2016, **2020**   978-1-988351-10-0
My Lousy Life Stories   2014, **2020**   978-1-988351-09-4
Persian Suns   **2021**   978-1-988351-15-5

Other (Artistic/Archival)   ISBN

About My Books   2016, 2022, **2025**   978-1-988351-20-9
About My Paintings   2022, **2025**   978-1-988351-17-9
The Stories behind My Photographs   2023, **2025**   978-1-988351-18-6

Ordering the Books

(Use the books' ISBNs for getting the latest editions)
For these books' most economical prices, order at **Amazon.ca**
Available also at Amazon.com and some bookstores,
as well as international markets

 erosbooks2020@gmail.com (for comments and contacting the author)

---

[*] Enhanced Editions of 12 older books were printed in 2020. They were resubmitted to the Library and Archives Canada Cataloguing as well. If a book's 'print date' on the copyright page is older, the newest version is available at Amazon and bookstores.

[1, 2] These two books are complementary in terms of humanity topics.

Table of Contents

List of Paintings
Author's Note
Introduction *1*
About Mosquito Creek Trail *4*
About the Lost Lagoon Set *7*
A Special Bond with the Black Swan! *10*
The Sudden Urge for Painting *21*
The Sneaky Tulip *28*
Simple Facts about Painting *29*
The Chairs Rivalry *33*
Behind the Scene (Part One) *33*
Painting Portraits *44*
Four Condemned Paintings *54*
The Play of Shadows *58*
Sharing a Sad Secret with a Seagull *59*
My Endless Eccentricities *62*
The Transition Dilemma *73*
The Meaning and Value of Art *77*
Flirting with My Muse *79*
A Beginner's Paintings *81*
Abstract Painting Popularity *83*
A Reconstructed Painting *87*
Behind the Scene (Part Two) *89*

Appendix A: A Major Reason for Transition to Writing *94*
Appendix B: A Conservative Suggested Price List for Paintings *95*

List of Paintings

Name	Medium	Size (inches)	Page
1. Howe Sound	Acrylic on Canvas	20 X 24	Front Cover
2. Self-portrait 2006	Oil on Canvas	24 X 20	Back Cover
3. Yosemite Tree I	Oil on Canvas	40 X 30	3
4. Mosquito Creek 1	Oil on Canvas	28 X 22	4
5. Mosquito Creek 2	Oil on Canvas	28 X 22	5
6. A View of Howe Sound	Oil on Canvas	36 X 48	6
7. Lost Lagoon 4	Oil on Canvas	36 X 48	6
8. Lost Lagoon Set, 1	Oil on Canvas	48 X 36	7
9. Lost Lagoon Set, 2	Oil on Canvas	48 X 36	8
10. Lost Lagoon Set, 3	Oil on Canvas	48 X 36	9
Lost Lagoon Set Options A&B	Oil on Canvas	48 X 108	8 and 9
11. Life's Oddities	Acrylic on Canvas	24 X 24	10
12. San Francisco Hills at Dusk	Oil on Canvas	30 X 40	11
13. Poppy Field	Oil on Canvas	36 X 54	11
14. Stanley Park Hills	Oil on Canvas	36 X 18	12
15. Lonesome Tree II	Oil on Canvas	36 X 18	13
16. Mosquito Creek 3 (MC)	Acrylic on Canvas	24 X 20	14
17. Secret Path at Mosquito Creek	Oil on Canvas	40 X 30	15
18. Water Lilies 1	Oil on Canvas	30 X 24	16
19. Water Lilies 2	Oil on Canvas	48 X 36	17
20. Edmonton Park 1	Oil on Canvas	40 X 30	18
21. Water Lilies 3	Oil on Canvas	30 X 24	19
22. Tanning in Nice 1	Oil on Canvas	40 X 30	20
23. Edmonton Park 2	Oil on Canvas	18 X 24	20
24. Dusk Mood in a Wide Field	Acrylic on Canvas	16 X 20	21
25. Yosemite Tree II	Oil on Canvas	28 X 22	23
26. Kenmore Creek	Acrylic on Canvas	28 X 22	24
27. Mosquito Creek 4	Oil on Canvas	24 X 20	25
28. Pacific Ocean from Whytecliff Park	Acrylic on Canvas	21½ X 35½	25
29. Silhouette	Oil on Canvas	36 X 24	26
30. Spring in Mountains	Oil on Canvas	30 X 40	27
31. Yosemite Field II	Oil on Canvas	24 X 30	27
32. A Cozy Corner at the Gallery	Oil on Canvas	30 X 24	28
33. Sneaky Tulip	Oil on Acrylic on Canvas	14 X 11	28
34. Alberta Park 1	Oil on Canvas	28 X 22	29
35. Banff, Alberta 1	Oil on Canvas	43 X 38	30
36. Banff, Alberta 2	Oil on Canvas	48 X 38	31
37. Jean Pierre's Living Room	Acrylic on Canvas	24 X 18	32
38. My Dinning Room	Acrylic on Canvas	22 X 28	32
39. Shadows Ambience	Oil on Canvas	20 X 16	34
40. Lights and Reflections	Oil on Canvas	20 X 16	34
41. Lost Lagoon's Bridge	Oil on Canvas	24 X 24	34
42. Pacific Ocean at Dusk	Oil on Canvas	30 X 40	32
43. Wandering Geese in Stanley Park (View from West Vancouver 1)	Oil on Canvas	20 X 16	35
44. Cherry Blossoms in MC Path	Oil on Canvas	20 X 16	36

List of Paintings (Cont.)

Name	Medium	Size (inches)	Page
45. Triumph in Unisom	Oil on Canvas	24 X 24	36
46. Puddle on the Path 1	Acrylic on Canvas	20 X 16	37
47. Yosemite Field I	Oil on Canvas	24 X 20	38
48. Reflections in Sausalito	Oil on Canvas	29 X 52	38
49. Solitude	Acrylic on Canvas	14 X 11	39
50. Cherry Blossoms in Stanley Park	Oil on Canvas	30 X 48	39
51. Tswassen Creek	Oil on Canvas	48 X 30	40
52. The White Cliff	Oil on Canvas	42 X 32	41
53. Edmonton Park 3	Oil on Canvas	40 X 30	42
54. K for Kudos to Nature	Oil on Canvas	28 X 22	42
55. T for Triumph	Oil on Canvas	30 X 24	42
56. Leaning Bell Tower, Venice	Oil on Canvas	42 X 32	43
57. Mosquito Creek Runoff	Oil on Canvas	22 X 28	43
58. Dusk at Lost Lagoon	Oil on Canvas	16 X 20	44
59. Pavarotti 1	Oil on Canvas	30 X 40	46
60. Pavarotti 2	Oil on Canvas	24 X 24	46
61. Nima 1	Oil on Canvas	16 X 16	47
62. Nima 2	Oil on Canvas	12 X 12	47
63. I Scream 2	Oil on Canvas	22 X 28	48
64. Persian Moons	Oil on Canvas	24 X 18	48
65. Colours of Romance	Acrylic on Canvas	28 X 22	49
66. Bowen Island & Howe Sound 1	Oil on Canvas	24 X 24	50
67. Bowen Island & Howe Sound 2	Oil on Canvas	24 X 24	50
68. Bowen Island & Howe Sound 3	Oil on Canvas	24 X 24	51
Bowen Island & Howe Sound, Set	Oil on Canvas	24 X 72	47
69. Path at Stanley Park 1	Oil on Canvas	24 X 36	52
70. Field in Alberta 1	Oil on Canvas	16 X 20	52
71. Edmonton Park 4	Oil on Canvas	40 X 30	53
72. Caspian Sea	Oil on Canvas	28 X 22	54
73. Puddle on the Path 2	Oil on Canvas	24 X 20	54
74. Battle of Light and Shadows at MC	Oil on Canvas	30 X 40	55
75. Colours at Mosquito Creek (MC)	Oil on Canvas	24 X 36	55
76. Field in Alberta 2	Oil on Canvas	11 X 14	56
77. Neighbour's Backyard	Oil on Canvas	24 X 30	56
78. Pacific Ocean at Dusk (View from West Vancouver 2)	Oil on Canvas	30 X 40	57
79. Dusk at West Vancouver Hills	Acrylic on Canvas	16 X 20	57
80. Tree Shadows at Whytecliff Park	Oil on Canvas	30 X 20	58
81. Sharing the Sad News with a Seagull	Oil on Canvas	16 X 20	59
82. A Path at West Vancouver	Oil on Canvas	24 X 20	59
83. Shannon Falls	Acrylic on Canvas	28 X 22	59
84. Mood in Lost Lagoon	Oil on Canvas	18 X 24	60
85. Moonlight at Lost Lagoon	Oil on Canvas	20 X 24	60
86. Last Rays at Yosemite	Oil on Canvas	22 X 28	61
87. Last Rays at English Bay, Vancouver	Oil on Canvas	20 X 24	61
88. Path at Stanley Park 2	Oil on Canvas	20 X 24	62
89. Checking the Grounds	Acrylic on Canvas	28 X 22	63

List of Paintings (Cont.)

Name	Medium	Size (inches)	Page
90. Barn in California	Oil on Canvas	16 X 20	64
91. Alberta Field	Oil on Canvas	16 X 20	64
92. Sunset Colours	Oil on Canvas	16 X 20	64
93. Sunflowers	Oil on Canvas	16 X 20	65
94. Yosemite Field 3	Acrylic on Canvas	16 X 20	66
95. Snow	Oil on Canvas	28 X 22	66
96. Fog	Oil on Canvas	28 X 22	66
97. Sunbathing in Nice 2	Oil on Canvas	20 X 16	67
98. Colours of a Creek	Oil on Canvas	24 X 20	67
99. Alberta Rockies 1	Oil on Canvas	18 X 24	67
100. Ducks' Manoeuvre at Lost Lagoon	Oil on Canvas	11 X 14	68
101. Lucky Fence	Oil on Canvas	11 X 14	68
102. Crushing Waves of Pacific Ocean	Oil on Acrylic on Canvas	16 X 20	69
103. A River in Alberta	Oil on Canvas	16 X 20	69
104. Lake in Whistler, BC	Oil on Canvas	16 X 20	70
105. Dusk at Lost Lagoon 2	Oil on Canvas	16 X 20	70
106. Juliet's *Original* Balcony!	Oil on Canvas	20 X 16	71
107. Lions Gate Bridge	Oil on Acrylic on Canvas	22 X 28	71
108. Yosemite Field 4	Oil on Canvas	30 X 48	72
109. Lagoon at Whistler	Oil on Canvas	20 X 24	72
110. Lost Lagoon 5	Oil on Canvas	24 X 30	73
111. Around Mosquito Creek	Oil on Acrylic on Canvas	20 X 16	75
112. Lush Green Field in BC	Oil on Canvas	22 X 28	76
113. Feeding the Birds	Oil on Canvas	20 X 16	76
114. Creek in Alberta	Oil on Canvas	20 X 16	76
115. Winter in the Country	Acrylic on Canvas	20 X 16	77
116. Spring in Vancouver	Oil on Canvas	20 X 16	79
117. Tree Rows	Acrylic on Canvas	28 X 22	79
118. Shadowy Sidewalk	Acrylic on Canvas	28 X 22	79
119. Seagulls at Stanley Park	Acrylic on Canvas	20 X 16	80
120. Lost Lagoon 6	Acrylic on Canvas	30 X 40	80
121. Lost Lagoon 7	Oil on Acid/Free Archival Paper	9 X 12	81
122. California Hills	Oil on Acid/Free Archival Paper	12 X 16	82
123. Cherry Blossoms at Stanley Park 2	Oil on Acid/Free Archival Paper	12 X 18	82
124. Lights and Shadows	Oil on Canvas	20 X 24	83
125. A Fish, Turtle, Bird, Snake, or Whale	Oil on Acid/Free Archival Paper	11 X 16	85
126. Endless Crash at Pacific Ocean	Oil on Acid/Free Archival Paper	9 X 12	85
127. An Orderly Flight at Sunset	Oil on Acid/Free Archival Paper	9 X 12	86
128. Alberta Rockies 3	Oil on Acid/Free Archival Paper	11 X 14	86
129. Waterfall	Oil on Acid/Free Archival Paper	12 X 9	86
130. A Tiny Creek in Whistler	Oil on Acid/Free Archival Paper	12 X 9	86
131. Sunset at West Vancouver	Oil on Acid/Free Archival Paper	12 X 18	86
132. Alberta Rockies 2	Oil on Acid/Free Archival Paper	9 X 12	86
133. A Forest Mood	Oil on Canvas	50 X 75	88
134. Path to Heaven	Oil on Canvas	40 X 30	93

Author's Note
and Acknowledgments

It is just baffling how my deep, ten-year passion for painting was dampened some 15 years ago by a sudden urge to write academic books and novels. In the hindsight, particularly, this switch feels weird, since, i) people and experts were encouraging me to keep painting and exhibiting them even more seriously, ii) many interesting ideas and subjects for painting, especially the bullfighting photo, #41, in *The Stories behind my Photographs* book, were singeing my brain for attention, and, III) painting had become my only source of relaxation and bearing my family and work problems.

Then again, the switch to writing had felt like a mission in line with my sense of duty to give my children a truer picture of life's harsh realities, while my angst about family relationships, societies' health, and humanity had been escalating. The expected, natural means of communication with my kids had been gradually abolished as well, rather in line with new society's naive zeal to spoil children, which is only ruining their characters and future in faltering societies. In fact, this parental conundrum alone makes the matter of addressing the sad state of humanity a global mission, as social sicknesses are now accelerating beyond control and ruining humans' mental capacities and lifestyles. Lots of research and essays are urgent just in hopes of eluding humans' looming demise. This concern will consume plenty of my time and energy in the next decade as well, if my health and stamina warrant the opportunity of writing a few more books. They will keep stressing on the same themes and goals noted in the booklet, *About My Books,* with even more emphasis on humanity. Sequels for the published novels, *Midnight Gate-opener* and *Persian Suns,* are also likely, although all these novels' goal have mainly been to demonstrate the growing decline of social and family health, anyway.

Meanwhile, publishing my paintings' images in a book had felt useful for keeping at least a public record of them, as I have become concerned about their fate with my departure to heaven getting closer. At least their existence should be acknowledged now that the likelihood of ever getting the urge and energy to do any more paintings or exhibitions is too low. I have also felt guilty for hoarding them when some experts and people visiting me made kind comments about them, while the idea of not having them around me (selling) them has felt unbearable, too—*maybe idiotically or wisely.*

The chance of revisiting many paintings that had been stacked up around the house has also been a great delight, thanks to my mysterious muse for cultivating the idea of preparing this book, too, although she might have been partly trying to make up for her role in pushing me switch to writing fifteen years ago. She has always been inspirational behind the scene, or maybe just fooling me to keep writing! At the same time, her persistence to discuss humanity even in this book further complicated the task of photographing 134 paintings and trying to remember their locales as well as my sentiments at the time. I had not imagined that composing even a picture book would take so much time and effort, all thanks to her again!

A few other people whose literary expertise I have valued, including my son, have never found time or interest to read my books' drafts and offer their inputs. Still, I would like to thank them as well for making me laugh and ponder humanity—even by their apathy—almost as much as my muse does.

Tom Omidi, Ph.D.
Vancouver, 2023, 2025

Introduction

The paintings depicted in this book reflect my artistic efforts to remain resilient during a perplexing/depressing period when both my career and marriage had felt doomed. Soon, this new hobby at the age of fifty had turned into a soothing obsession like a sacred mission for healing. Then, I stopped somewhat abruptly ten years later when the chances of words expressing my convoluted sentiments felt better and easier. This turnaround was in 2006, almost after painting the self-portrait printed on the back cover. Perhaps staring long hours at those glaring eyes and the cynical smirk I was planting in the portrait had made me realize how pathetic my life had become, as hinted in my other books amid humorous stories for showing life's ironies.

The idea of archiving the paintings had dawned on me in recent years, too, as I had stopped showing them in galleries in order to focus on writing. These paintings also deserved my big gratitude for boosting my spirit and stamina during the last two gloomy, adventurous decades, especially for writing books zealously. Thus, finally, I started this book at the expense of putting my ongoing writing projects, especially the ones about humanity, on hold. Luckily, this book's new edition is happening after the planned main book, i.e., *Humans Versus Humanity*, has been published just recently.

Then, including some background and stories about the paintings or my altering passions felt inevitable as well, even at the risk of parading the depth of my senility or naïveté at this age in line with my accelerating gloom about humanity. For one thing, justifying even our artistic efforts and books about art is now getting harder within the current social climate. Instead, dissecting the world we have created for ourselves is becoming highly urgent due to the fast downfall of society and leadership along with rising human idiocies that transpire also in my naive character and futile hopes about humans' chance for salvation. Sadly, it is getting harder not to whine desolately about the growing global hardships, unrests, foolish choices, and humanity's dire prospects all due to humans' pitiful power struggles, pomposity, ignorance, crude ambitions, evil plans, and greedy mentalities leading to irreversible global calamities, especially the rampant climate crisis. In particular, it is excruciating to witness our conceited leaders looking so numb, dumb, and casual about the impracticality of current social systems and their selfish deeds. These fundamentals also question the rationality and purpose of art as well as many other of humans' professional and recreational endeavours. This ironic, philosophical topic is reviewed deeper later in this book.

In all, discussing modern world's harsh realities felt useful to both augment some images' messages and goad more people ponder and push radical changes needed in our faltering social and personal mentalities. Perhaps some people would also read my books, which mainly present the facts about the sad states of societies and family relationships, to get a finer sense about the way modernism is crippling humans. Our current approach to focus only on symptoms of social problems, while ignoring the main roots of our looming demise deliberately, especially capitalism, is futile.

Although every picture is allegedly worth a thousand words, in this special case, this book's images alone could not depict how badly human arrogance and ignorance are damaging Nature and humanity. While these simple landscape images can best depict the glory of Nature, only words *might* reflect the ugliness that human mentality has imposed on the universe. Not even a thousand pictures can ever capture the vast contrast between humans' and Nature's needs.

Besides mitigating the monotony of just flipping through so many pictures, words might also help some caring readers gather a fairer sense of my stoic attitude, rather than trusting only people's crude judgments about a lost human with a bizarre, radical attitude! You now also learn firsthand how my muse makes me whine so much in my books and expose my convoluted mentality so readily. Then again, the privilege of communicating with thoughtful readers has in itself turned into a new obsession for me now after giving up painting, my marriage, and my boring job with the government to delve into writing fifteen years ago.

Ironically, while painting had most likely instigated my interest in writing, it had in itself been a derivative of my long obsession with photography since adolescence after my father had given me his beloved Zeiss Ikon camera along with an urge to capture expressive moods and images. It had soon turned into a serious, soothing hobby in a setting that had already given me a bad taste about the purpose and meaning of life even as a child, especially when God imposes a dysfunctional family on us to grow up in. This early attraction and exposure to nature had certainly played a big role in forming my character and passions for painting and writing, as well as other smaller interests, such as gardening.

My urge for capturing the beauty and messages of nature had grown after we arrived in scenic Vancouver forty years ago. Our calm surroundings simply enthralled me, especially when life in quiet North Vancouver rendered the opportunity of taking thousands of pictures during my afternoon walks in the Mosquito Creek Park. Then, building a professional colour darkroom at home availed the opportunity of printing many of those splendid scenes in large format. Photography had helped me manage my life better in line with a bearable perspective around a family that had kept whining more every day, instead of appreciating my efforts to love and support them, while my dull employment also singed my spirit. Then, the sudden urge to start painting some of those pictures at the age of fifty had put a big dent in my first artistic obsession—photography.

Still, most of the paintings depicted in this book are from the landscape photos I had taken around the world, especially in Canada, for forty years. Some subjects, such as trees and creeks, and some locations, such as Lost Lagoon in Stanley Park, Mosquito Creek Park in North Vancouver, and Yosemite Park have received the highest emphasis mostly by the way they had absorbed me and also resulted in my favourite paintings. All along, my chronic curiosity had encouraged me experiment with many styles to depict nature's moods in my paintings, although a semblance of impressionism had always prevailed. By the way, these paintings are not varnished.

The List of Paintings outlining the 134 images is mainly for reference in this and other likely books, especially the one about the photographs behind these paintings. Now, those photos suddenly seem to have their own rights for a mention and archival purposes, too, along with amusing stories during my long photography adventures, including my amusing, artistic rivalry with my dear dad during my adolescence. I miss my peculiar dad and our humorous, bizarre encounters, as recounted partially in my novel Midnight Gate-opener, but a bit in this book as well. The Table of Contents can help in finding some touchy topics and stories deemed useful for this picture book.

Naming the paintings proved a difficult task in itself, as recalling the locations and dates of many pictures taken ages ago became a challenge, while explaining nature's special mood, romance, colour, or light had also felt vital. So, forgive any likely errors about their locations, while naming them properly with a hint about their backgrounds had oddly felt also essential. Old age has escalated my eccentricities somewhat, too, after all! Particularly, naming a few abstracts, especially painting # 63, *I scream 2*, based on intuition per se was amusing, in line with a huge urge to imagine and state my personal sentimentality along with a possible story behind them, or merely reflect my intention and grasp of those abstract paintings!

3. Yosemite Tree 1, Oil on Canvas, 40 X 30 inches (based on photo #19)

Most of the paintings inspired by a photograph include the related photos' numbers, as listed in *The Stories behind my Photographs* book in case some readers wish to compare them. Still, many paintings without a photo # have most likely been based on some of my photographs as well, although I have not been able to find and include them in the book mentioned above or show a reference for them in this book.

4. Mosquito Creek 1, Oil on Canvas, 28 X 22 (based on photo # 22)

About Mosquito Creek Trail

For 10-15 years, I had hiked a portion of Mosquito Creek trail in North Vancouver a few times weekly and taken hundreds of pictures of its tranquil mood. A dozen times,

I had even hiked all the way down and up this long, steep trail for a serious exercise or reflection. This routine has faded in the last decade gradually, though.

5. Mosquito Creek 2, Oil on Canvas, 28 X 22 (based on photo # 23)

Ironically, most of my paintings stress on the trail's trees, except for paintings # 74 and 75 that provide a wide view of the Creek itself. (See also the note at the bottom of page 54.)

6. A View of Howe Sound, Oil on Canvas, 36 X 48 (based on photo # 121)

7. Lost Lagoon 4, Oil on Canvas, 36 X 48 (based on photo # 46)

About the Lost Lagoon Set

The Lost Lagoon paintings #8-10 constitute a set with the idea of offering a wide view of the birds' busy life in such an exquisite surrounding in the Vancouver's Stanley Park, where I frequented often and took many pictures. The set has been designed to be mixed in any order and provide all six possible combinations (varieties), while ensuring the edges connect rather perfectly in all combinations. Option A and B are shown on pages 8 and 9 as examples. Any one or a mix of two of these paintings can also be displayed separately, thus rendering 13 options in total—*plus, of course, the option of hiding some or all of them in a vault merely for investment or something, like what has become so customary, nowadays!*

8. Lost Lagoon Set, 1, Oil on Canvas, 48 X 36 (based on photo # 27)

9. Lost Lagoon Set, 2, Oil on Canvas, 48 X 36 (based on photo # 28)

Option A of the six possible combinations

10. Lost Lagoon Set, 3, Oil on Canvas, 48 X 36 (based on photo # 29)

Option B of the six possible combinations

A Special Bond with the Black Swan!

My regular outings to Stanley Park and taking the pictures of those purposeful, beautiful birds also made me contemplate life and my confused being. Ironically, I also felt deeply for the lonely black swan depicted in painting #9, especially when the duo, showy white swans cuddled so romantically and snubbed us sneakier every time to make us envious. In return, the black swan and I gradually grew a peculiar bond and I included only it in my paintings, though I took many pictures of the white swans, too. Now, I wish I had painted those charming white swans as well, instead of only mocking their showy manoeuvres. They looked so devoted to each other and those love scenes could have made perfect paintings. *Silly me!*

Nevertheless, I went to those birds' sanctuary regularly rather masochistically to mourn my loneliness, while the sad black swan seemed to be pitying me with its curious red eyes as well, as if sensing my growing confusion about both of us by the way I appeared so pensive those days due to my family's insensitive attitude. Then, I even concocted a funny story about those wily swans and included it in my abstract novel, *My Lousy Life Stories,* in the chapter called *the Pink Dove*.

11. Life's Oddities, Acrylic on Canvas, 24 X 24

12. San Francisco Hills at Dusk, Oil on Canvas, 30 X 40 (based on photo # 110)

13. Poppy Field, Oil on Canvas, 36 X 54

14. Stanley Park Hills, Oil on Canvas, 36 X 18 (from photo # 77)

15. Lonesome Tree II, Oil on Canvas, 36 X 18 (from photo # 76)

16. Mosquito Creek 3 (MC), Acrylic on Canvas, 24 X 20 (from photo # 24)

17. Secret Path at Mosquito Creek, Oil on Canvas, 40 X 30 (based on photo # 171)

18. Water Lilies 1, Oil on Canvas, 30 X 24 (based on photo # 93)

19. Water Lilies 2, Oil on Canvas, 30 X 24 (based on photo # 95)

20. Edmonton Park 1, Oil on Canvas, 40 X 30 (based on photo # 152)

21. Water Lilies 3, Oil on Canvas, 48 X 36 (based on photo # 98)

22. Tanning in Nice 1, Oil on Canvas, 40 X 30 (based on photo # 138)

23. Edmonton Park 2, Oil on Canvas, 18 X 24

24. Dusk Mood in a Wide Field, Acrylic on Canvas, 16 X 20 (Lower Mainland, Vancouver)

The Sudden Urge for Painting

A sudden urge to start painting struck me in one gloomy afternoon when I drove to Whytecliff Park in West Vancouver, gazed into the romantic scenery in the horizon, and pondered the pains of existence. The full story of this event and my ecstatic mood in that moment is recounted in my abstract novel, *My Lousy Life Stories,* in the chapter called *Howe Sound.* An excerpt from that chapter about that evoking scenery is reprinted here in case you wish to compare the words I had used to describe my mood at that moment with the painting I eventually did of that scene (Howe Sound, Front Cover.) A photograph, #57, from that scene with some resemblance to the painting on Front Cover is also printed in the book, *Stories behind My Photograph.*

………

A gloomy day… A big cluster of dark, loaded clouds crowds the cobalt sky. A shapely interlaced mountain formation in the horizon resembles a line of steppingstones over the ocean linking Bowen Island to Horseshoe Bay. A pinkish haze saturates the colours of plantations dressing the mountains. Another mix of glorifying hues diffuses some violet rays on the cloud tufts, and scatters a soft, soothing reflection over the Bay. A few glitters of purple and ultramarine mingle merely a touch above the water, making a vast area of the ocean appear solid like a china dish. Jeremy imagines a stone striking the surface of the water would only clink and bounce a few times before settling smoothly on the glistening ocean surf. Far out, near the horizon, a tiny sailboat stands still like a *white dot* in the middle of the vast universe. At that moment, Howe Sound resembles the whole universe to him, with the wee white dot further exaggerating its glory and enigma. Then again, the overwhelming ambiance, including the menacing clouds, is reverently romantic.

He wonders why the sailboat is out there in this weather and who is inside it. In a fleeting trance, he imagines himself all alone in the boat's cabin at the centre of the universe. The image surges another wave of serenity within him. A shallow breeze rustles the nearby leaves and branches, and he believes the clouds shuffled slightly, too.

He gazes at the scenery for another half an hour, until the daylight dies and gradually the horizon becomes a blur. He can hardly discern the formation of the mountains or the location of the boat. He hopes that whoever is in the cabin is safe and knows what he is doing out there this late with a storm possibly gushing in the Bay any minute. A fantastic thought enters his mind: Maybe a man and a woman in the cabin are so deeply in love they do not realize what time it is, how fast the light has faded, and how dangerous a sudden storm may be. Or maybe they know, but their love is so powerful they do not care about the consequences, not even if they die in each other's arms that very instant. He wishes he were the man.

But he is not the lucky man, and it is now time for him to go home, back to reality, in the bosom of his nagging wife. He moves away from the edge of the cliff carefully, as his body feels numb after sitting in one spot for so long. But his mind is clear now: Suicide is out of the question and arguing with Lorie must stop. He should simply learn to tolerate the situation even more than before. Now he has more energy and spiritual wisdom to control his ego and temper. He must also commit himself to paint the scenery he has engraved into the deepest channels of his brain so diligently. He must paint the scenery that seems to have changed his perspective so swiftly and made him feel alive again. But how? He is not a landscape painter, he reminds himself again in the car, driving home with a grin cracking all over his face. *Yes, yes, I must learn 'perfection' and I will paint that scenery when I am ready. I must do it to survive. I will.*

……

Although the above romantic mood had triggered my passion for painting in line with the details noted in the *Howe Sound* story, in *My Lousy Life Stories,* I did not dare, for a year or so, to tackle the scene imprinted in my head. Thus, exhibiting it on the front cover felt quite appropriate, as much as the self-portrait did for the back cover, **as reminders of the beginning and the end of my painting obsession!**

By the way, I had painted an imaginary scene some twenty years earlier in Iowa when visiting my brother, Nick, while waiting for the long process of my family's immigration to Canada. My stress from boredom away from my beloved young family had kept growing along with many hallucinations about the task of rebuilding a life in a new environment during the early 1980's big recession. Then, a strange dream one night was followed by a strong urge to paint its main scene during the long hours I was left alone in Nick's suite. Anyway, I acted upon this bizarre urge and painted a mediocre large canvas that I left for Nick when he seemed to like it more than I did. Still, the image and story itself stayed in my subconscious until I painted a portrait called *Persian Moons* twenty years later, which happens to be a derivative of the first painting I had done in Iowa based on my weird dream. Then, I wrote a novel, *Persian Moons,* 6-7 years later about the whole thing, i.e., a likely lover's story in my dream. In the novel, the original painting is called the *Woman in the White Dress* and it plays a major role in the events transpiring in the story. The painting shows a pensive man looking out the window at a mysterious woman in a long white dress lingering on the sandy beach desolately and staring at the ship disappearing in the wide horizon. The *Persian Moons* portrait, painting #64, shows a dreamy woman sitting in a gazebo, while a man is running outside in the dark beach towards her. I wish I had at least a picture of the *Woman in the White Dress* to include in this book. Where are you, Nick, my weird, dear brother?

25. Yosemite Tree II, Oil on Canvas, 28 X 22 (based on photo # 73)

26. Kenmore Creek, Acrylic on Canvas, 28 X 22

27. Mosquito Creek 4, Oil on Canvas, 24 X 20

28. Pacific Ocean from Whytecliff Park, Acrylic on Canvas, 21½ X 35½ (from photo # 122)

29. Silhouette, Oil on Canvas, 36 X 24 (based on photo # 80)

30. Spring in Mountains, Oil on Canvas, 30 X 40 (based on photo # 70)

31. Yosemite Field II, Oil on Canvas, 24 X 30 (based on photo # 20)

32. A Cozy Corner at the Gallery, Oil on Canvas, 30 X 24 (based on photo # 164)

The Sneaky Tulip

This tricky tulip had grabbed my attention and I had taken its picture after my clownish mind had insisted that it had been trying to imitate an orchid or pretending to be one! Maybe it had imagined that by opening up and revealing its inner self, people would love it even more. To me, however, its beauty almost matched an orchid's already without taking the hassle of flaunting so idiotically. Maybe humans are not the only species so adamant to show off, after all! Even if the tulip's deformation had been merely the result of an accident or misfortune, it still deserved some kind of tribute for its dainty pose, I reckoned. Therefore, I even painted the large original photo of the tulip that I had printed myself and hung in the drawing room for years.

33. Sneaky Tulip, Oil on Acrylic, from photo #159

34. Alberta Park 1, Oil on Canvas, 28 X 22 (based on photo # 151)

<u>Simple Facts about Painting</u>
While photographing the paintings for this book personally, some images' quality did not look perfect due to lighting and editing deficiencies. This exercise also showed how both the changes in a viewer's mood and the light source on or around every painting (even by minute variations) make it manifest and affect the same person rather differently. These simple factors alone, besides the needed talent, makes painting an exacting task, and often frustrating, almost like writing, for fussy painters

and writers who have difficulty accepting their works final for a long time or ever. Luckily, I could stop fussing over the pictures' qualities after convincing myself that the main goal of this book has been to archive my paintings, though including lots of *enlightening* words about them, *like this page's weird remarks,* had felt useful, too!

Another interesting discovery, while taking some paintings off their frames for photographing them, was that they look much nicer in the frame! We all imagine this fact, but the effect seems much bigger than we, especially a painter, expect naturally. Then, I wondered if that was true for my frameless large paintings as well. A few finer facts about paintings are noted in the upcoming sections.

35. Banff, Alberta 1, Oil on Canvas, 43 X 38 (based on photo # 154)

36. Banff, Alberta 2, Oil on Canvas, 48 X 38 (based on photo # 153)

37. Jean Pierre's Living Room, Acrylic on Canvas, 24 X 18 (based on photo # 157)

38. My Dinning Room, Acrylic on Canvas, 22 X 28 (based on photo # 158)

The Chairs Rivalry

I visited Jean Pierre and Jackie in Bordeaux in the summer of 1980 and took a picture of their living room, as it had looked particularly cozy to me. J.P. and I had become good friends and visited each other's countries after being classmates at USC in Los Angeles in the early 1970's. Many years later, I painted that photograph when the Federation of Canadian Artists announced a competition for its members, which had to include a chair, a newspaper, and a pear. All I had to do was to add a pear and a newspaper, which I decided to put on the chair. To me, it suggests that the chair's occupant, possibly Jean Pierre, had been called away abruptly while reading his paper and taking a bite of his pear.

"What do you want now, Jackie," he might've yelled at his wife with frustration.

After the painting was accepted for exhibition and then returned to me, I hung it in my dinning room to complement the eight chairs around the big table.

With my witty brain often trying to stir my sense of humour or fool me, soon I felt that the eight chairs in my dinning room were questioning my loyalty by painting and exhibiting J.P.'s chair (painting # 37) in a prominent gallery, instead of painting any of my own eight chairs that had been serving me for many years!!! Then, I had even hung it in the dinning room right above their heads. *'Take it out of* **our room** *at least, you ungrateful lout,'* they seemed to be yelling at me and amongst them sometimes.

A few times, I tickled about the idea of making it up to them somehow or at least move the painting out of the dinning room. Then, finally, one day a graceful scene manifested magically when the sunshine was flowing softly through the cherry tree outside the dinning room and spreading the top chair and curtain's shadows on the table. I took a picture giddily and painted it (#38) after adding the estranged wine glasses to the scene. The painting's interpretation is surely left to the viewers, yet I cannot resist the urge to share mine, which is dramatic, as usual. To me, a sneaky woman (maybe my ex-wife) is still sitting at the table and sipping her wine coolly with a triumphant smirk after her frustrated husband (maybe me) has smacked his wine glass and stormed out of the room when she had asked him for a divorce.

Behind the Scene (Part One)

Even this picture book has ironically incited plenty of *personal and philosophical reflections* about my seemingly erratic passions and professions, maybe as my dire idiosyncrasies. These kinds of self-analyses also revive our lingering dilemmas about the path of life that either we choose in line with our untamed personalities or the universe imposes upon us playfully, if not designedly! On the one hand, painting so zealously an entire decade—despite big professional and family obligations—had felt like a divine mission. It still does most often! On the other hand, letting my curiosities and passions stir such an adventurous, taxing existence has felt insane occasionally. Now, I just cannot believe my patience and drive for doing this many paintings in such details before turning to research and writing non-stop and getting fussier about the whole purpose of existence, too. Perhaps my life would have been simpler and easier without my lifelong academic and artistic curiosities inundating me, though a mystical force **often** appears to be goading many of us follow peculiar paths of life in line with our enigmatic visions and ambitions.

By the way, another amusing factor (mystery) about some particular paintings is their power to absorb us mysteriously way beyond the effect of large photographs of the same splendid scenery or portrait. Why do we get so mesmerized and stare at certain paintings for hours sometimes? Is it because the painters' souls manifest in those paintings? Even these simple life oddities or mysteries baffle us forever, as we analyse our thoughts and actions to define or grasp our beings. To avoid boring the readers, these crude observations are elaborated at the end of the book, page 89, only for those interested in psychological and philosophical discussions.

Luckily, at least this book has been finally completed after stopping myself from dwelling on life's mystifying ironies and the images' qualities!

39. Shadows Ambience, Oil on Canvas, 20 X 16

40. Lights and Reflections, Oil on Canvas, 20 X 16

41. Lost Lagoon's Bridge, Oil on Canvas, 24 X 24 (from photo # 167)

42. Pacific Ocean at Dusk, Oil on Canvas, 30 X 40 (View from West Vancouver 1) (based on photo # 108)

43. Wandering Geese in Stanley Park, Oil on Canvas, 20 X 16 (from photo #167)

44. Cherry Blossoms in Mosquito Creek Park, Oil on Canvas, 20 X 16 (based on photo # 162)

45. Triumph in Unisom, Oil on Canvas, 24 X 24

46. Puddle on the Path 1, Acrylic on Canvas, 20 X 16 (based on photo # 169)

47. Yosemite Field I, Oil on Canvas, 24 X 20

48. Reflections in Sausalito, Oil on Canvas, 29 X 52 (based on photo # 156)

49. Solitude, Acrylic on Canvas, 14 X 11

50. Cherry Blossoms in Stanley Park, Oil on Canvas, 30 X 48 (based on photo # 160)

51. Tswassen Creek, Oil on Canvas, 48 X 30

52. The Whyte Cliff, Oil on Canvas, 42 X 32

53. Edmonton Park 3, Oil on Canvas, 40 X 30

54. K for Kudos to Nature, Oil on Canvas, 28 X 22

55. T for Triumph, Oil on Canvas, 30 X 24

56. Leaning Bell Tower, Venice, Oil on Canvas, 42 X 32

57. Mosquito Creek Runoff, Oil on Canvas, 22 X 28

58. Dusk at Lost Lagoon, Oil on Canvas, 16 X 20

Painting Portraits

'How about painting some portraits now, if you dare?' my pesky curiosity insisted eventually. After failing to find a suitable subject for the project, the image shown in painting #64 emerged in my head along with a love story about the *Woman in the White Dress,* the painting mentioned in the last paragraph of page 22. The new portrait painting was named *Persian Moons* many years later and used for the cover of my first novel by the same title. In fact, the stories of the two paintings, *Persian Moons* and the *Woman in the White Dress,* mix nicely in that novel. Accordingly, it feels plausible that *Persian Moons* portrait had evolved in my head or dreams as a follow up to the story of the *Woman in the White Dress* or because I had missed the latter painting and wondered about its fate in the hands of my lost brother, Nick, or if that old painting still existed! Apparently, Nick has become a good painter himself now from what I hear, maybe due to the influence of the *Woman in the White Dress*, too!? It shows that even a serious, busy space physicist may get enticed by artistry, or possibly by the *Woman in the White Dress* per se!

All these romantic sentiments while painting *Persian Moons* had most likely also led to the idea of writing *Persian Moons*, my first novel. Therefore, the *Woman in the White Dress* and *Persian Moons* had also probably been responsible for distracting my passion for painting.

Still unable to find a more relevant subject, I painted Pavarotti's portraits as he appeared in operas often those days with his heavenly voice that eased my stress. Then, finally, after feeling lucky to have found a worthy subject to paint, I asked my son to let me take his pictures for doing his portrait. Surely, the idea of asking him to sit a few hours for this project had felt out of the question. Even the pictures he agreed to let me take showed his low patience with me at least and they did not seem quite suitable for a large format painting, either. Anyhow, I chose two of his best poses for the project just to keep my words. Most of all, I hoped that looking at his portraits, which are the exact replicas of the photos he let me take for this job, would make him notice how *every picture is worth a thousand words!*

The self-portrait on the back cover was the last portrait I did, which possibly put the final nail in my urge for painting as well, as noted in the first paragraph of the Introduction. I had tried to make my eyes in this self-portrait an effective venue for you to contact my soul, while I also keep an eye on things here forever. You will believe me if you see the actual painting in a museum or something, although my claim is a bit noticeable in the image on the back cover, too.

By the way, the abstract self-portrait painting #63, *I Scream 2,* is also one of my favourite works due to the subtle message I had hoped to instil in it about life's sad, emotional intricacies bringing us to our knees with lasting despair and confusion.

After doing these portraits, my sneaky brain insisted that it was time to graduate to the next level, which felt to be a nude painting. *Time to focus on body after doing enough weird faces*, my muse insisted. It would be the toughest, final challenge for becoming a real painter, I surmised lustfully, while composing a sketch of the setting for an exquisite nude painting. I could imagine how perfect it would look on a large canvas at the exact size of the gorgeous model.

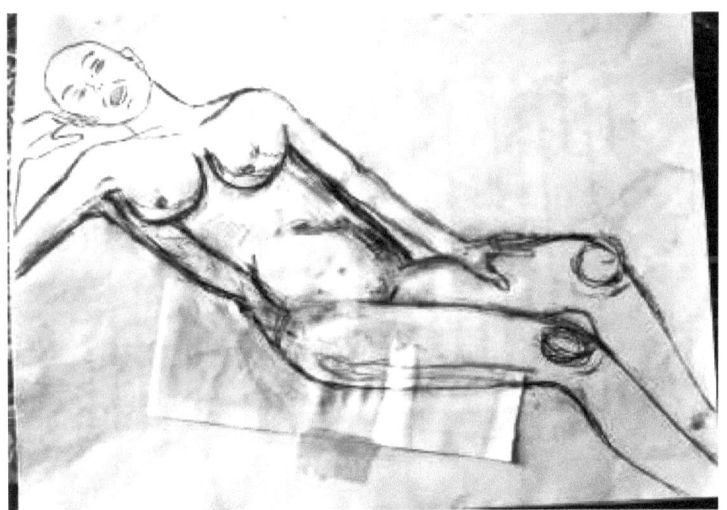

This nude sketch was also prepared with great hopes twenty years ago, but I am still waiting for a **gorgeous** model to jump right into it and make it come to life as my eternal masterpiece.

I did paintings #22 and #97 for practicing nude, anyway!

Sadly, though, I failed to convince an elegant, classy model with long, lustrous hair to pose naked for me for hours or let me take her nude photos for this sacred project. I did not like to paint anybody, the kind of seemingly loose models that old, famous painters had apparently been comfortable painting! Actually, as the sketch shows, I had decided to also check her long hair first specifically before designing it on her pretty body patiently as she laid there comfortably in the designed layout. *The long wait and my failure to find a perfect, cooperative model for the finest display of my artistry might have also affected my decision to switch to writing!*

Well, the opportunity to paint a special person's nude, if that gorgeous model with a long hair ever comes around, would probably offer the only incentive to pick up my brushes again after twenty years. **Any *perfect* volunteers hoping to challenge me, while also being eternalized?**

59. Pavarotti 1, Oil on Canvas, 30 X 40

60. Pavarotti 2, Oil on Canvas, 24 X 24

61. Nima 1, Oil on Canvas, 16 X 16

62. Nima 2, Oil on Canvas, 12 X 12

63. I Scream 2, Oil on Canvas, 22 X 28

64. Persian Moons, Oil on Canvas, 24 X 18

65. Colours of Romance, Acrylic on Canvas, 28 X 22 (based on photo # 163)

By the way, showing human figures in my landscape paintings had always felt gratuitous, if not outrageous, to me due to all the damage we have been inflicting on Nature, societies, and ourselves by our idiocies and helplessness, which are difficult moods to capture in a painting, anyway. Only paintings #65 and 134 contain symbolic human figures for their particular reasons. It is odd how we associate animals and plants with nature, but not humans! In fact, we are now totally anti-nature, and Nature does not want us, either!! Then again, Nature is not much human friendly, anyway, despite its splendour—very much like the concept of love.

66. Bowen Island & Howe Sound 1, Oil on Canvas, 24 X 24

67. Bowen Island & Howe Sound 2, Oil on Canvas, 24 X 24

68. Bowen Island & Howe Sound 3, Oil on Canvas, 24 X 24

Bowen Island & Howe Sound, Set, Oil on Canvas, 24 X 72 (See last three paintings)

69. Path at Stanley Park 1, Oil on Canvas, 24 X 36

70. Field in Alberta 1, Oil on Canvas, 16 X 20

71. Edmonton Park 4, Oil on Canvas, 40 X 30

Four Condemned Paintings

While gathering my paintings from various corners of the house to photograph for this book, I recalled the four I had exiled to the cold, dark garage many years earlier, as they had felt inadequate for my taste. Now, suddenly, it seemed timely to go check on them to finalize their fates and clear the crowded garage, too.

After finding, dusting, and carrying them upstairs, I kept looking at them with surprise, wondering why I had turned against these four paintings (#72-75) years ago particularly. Now, they did not appear more flawed or incomplete than most other paintings around me all along, which I was photographing eagerly to include in this book. In fact, I liked these four now, especially #74 & 75, while apologizing to them for my cruelty fifteen years earlier. All those cold winters in the garage, collecting dust and bearing my car fumes, had been so callous! At least I had shown enough sense to cover them with two layers of plastic bags.

How and why my rampant mood had turned me against these four paintings in particular made me wonder about human brains' capricious operation day to day. Yet, I could especially blame my urge for perfectionism for my cynical perspectives of my paintings and writings at any moment as well. Actually, my cynicism seems to be worsening and affecting my senses and decisions about everything, including the meaning of art in a doomed world or the purposes of our passions, our cruelties, and existence overall. These lingering dilemmas and doubts inflict us all largely in line with our psychological constructs, although they appear to burden our psyches faster and deeper every generation as humanity faces more impasses.

72. Caspian Sea, Oil on Canvas, 28 X 22

73. Puddle on the Path 2, Oil on Canvas, 24 X 20
(from photo # 169)

The following two pictures were most likely taken at Mosquito Creek Park, yet they could have actually been taken at Capilano River trail, which is only two kilometres west of Mosquito Creek Park. As much I craved and planned to hike these two trails again to detect the exact spot of these pictures, I could not gather the stamina to go so far down those trails and back during the period this book was being finalized.

74. Battle of Light and Shadows (Mosquito Creek?), Oil on Canvas, 30 X 40

75. Colours at MC (Mosquito Creek?), Oil on Canvas, 30 X 40

76. Field in Alberta 2, Oil on Canvas, 11 X 14

77. Neighbour's Backyard, Oil on Canvas, 24 X 30

78. Pacific Ocean at Dusk, Oil on Canvas, 30 X 40 (View from West Vancouver 2) (based on photo # 102)

79. Dusk at West Vancouver Hills, Acrylic on Canvas, 16 X 20

The Play of Shadows

I had taken the picture used for painting #80 when the shadows' prominence and precision on the trail—so dissimilar to the tree's format—had drawn my attention. In particular, the big curvy shadow on the path looks so outstanding compared to its source—the tiny curve in one branch near the top. Just some shadows exerting so much beauty, power, and enigma is simply amazing. In fact, shadows play a big role in the glory of nature, as depicted in many of my paintings, including #124. That is the play of Nature just for our amusement, I reckon with a spiritual sense! *Hooray!*

The original picture of this scene is printed in *Stories behind My Photographs*. It verifies the authenticity of the shadows' odd play in painting #80 as well. I changed the background in the original painting slightly a year or so later for some reason I do not remember now, but the shadows, as the main theme, are still intact.

80. Tree Shadows at Whytecliff Park, Oil on Canvas, 30 X 20 (from photo # 170)

Sharing a Sad Secret with a Seagull

I cannot fathom how this weird scenario and the idea of painting it had crossed my spooky brain! It was painted a few years before my marital conflicts had felt out of control, thus it could not have been the effect of divorce or loneliness. Then again, maybe my *clever* mind had felt my ex-wife's growing tension to build her guts and ask for a divorce soon! Moreover, sharing that sensitive secret with a seagull, rather than a friend perhaps, is even more enigmatic and interesting, as if I could not find or trust anybody to share my growing agony with. Of course, making the seagull look so keen, engaged, or nosy had been a big purpose of this painting as well, though it also looks funny. If you cannot read the note in the painting clearly, it says, "Dear Joe, I must go. I don't love you anymore. Mary."

I told the bird how happy and confused I had been that she'd at least called me "Dear," instead of using an insulting adjective like usual even in this damn note!

81. Sharing the Sad News with a Seagull, Oil on Canvas, 16 X 20

82. A Path at West Vancouver, Oil on Canvas, 24 X 20   83. Shannon Falls, Acrylic on Canvas, 28 X 22

84. Mood in Lost Lagoon, Oil on Canvas, 18 X 24

85. Moonlight at Lost Lagoon, Oil on Canvas, 20 X 24

86. Last Rays at Yosemite, Oil on Canvas, 22 X 28

87. Last Rays at English Bay, Vancouver, Oil on Canvas, 20 X 24 (based on photo # 61)

88. Path at Stanley Park 2, Oil on Canvas, 20 X 24

My Endless Eccentricities
My *enlightening* commentaries in this book have revealed many of my eccentricities already. Yet, confessing openly to a big one related to my paintings specifically would be useful: Along with the sudden urge to start painting, the idea of selling many of my *masterpieces* and becoming a renowned artist, had entertained me, too, the way all humans feel! Accordingly, I eventually applied and got accepted as an active member of the Federation of Canadian Artists. Then, I began presenting my paintings in the Federation's Gallery as well as galleries and exhibitions in Vancouver. Soon, though, I felt nostalgic when some paintings were sold. The sense of not seeing them ever again, especially my own favourites, like painting #120 shown on page 80, saddened me deeply after selling about a dozen paintings, like losing my only faithful kids when my family had already abandoned me so callously. Accordingly, I stopped exhibiting them and quit my membership in the Federation of Canadian Artists, while wondering what was wrong with me. *Gosh, I have really lost track of my eccentricities!*

Luckily, however, a profound philosophical notion soon supported my attitude: *What is the point of spending so much time and sentiment to paint a favourite subject and then spend more time and energy to give it away to a stranger just for money or fame, especially if you do not need or enjoy either of them?*

I also miss the painting I gave to my daughter who seemed drawn to it and the one I gave to a lost lover when she asked for it during our ceremonious separation! *The nerve of her, ha?! Why people are drawn so specifically only to some paintings, like the way my daughter and ex-lover had, remains another mystery for me.* Sadly, I had not taken good pictures of these two paintings and those sold in galleries or I cannot find them, except for the painting #120 on page 80, which was sold quickly at the Federation of Canadian Artists' Gallery to go a stranger's house. Luckily, I found a snapshot of the one my daughter has and made a decent photo of it, #124.

I wish I could contact the new owners and ask for a picture of those paintings. In particular, I wished, but felt no guts or conviction, to contact and ask my daughter for a picture of the painting or whether she liked to show it off in this book. I just did not want to bother the family who has forsaken me so casually.

Overall, I have apparently completed around 150 paintings during that gloomy decade devoted to this sacred mission, which means around 1.3 small and large paintings per month. It feels like a good achievement, *especially since 12 to 120 of them are masterpieces, I reckon humbly!* Thus, preparing a sample suggested price for the first 38 paintings on the List of Paintings and my two favourites felt useful, at least for minimizing experts and investors' pains trying to guess their real values after my departure. *Such a nice guy I am!* The list appears on the last page, Appendix B. Of course, you can always contact me or my agent for other paintings' best prices.

By way, I used a regular plate for palette to mix pigments, while my ex-wife screamed about the matter. It was a good enough tool and worked fine with no need for a palette. Thus, a picture of my painting plate and gloves is shown here as a token of my big gratitude for their long service. Still, maybe my act of stealing the second plate, after the first one was ruined, had contributed to my ex-wife's final resolve to ask me for a divorce!!

89. Checking the Grounds, Acrylic on Canvas, 28 X 22

90. Barn in California, Oil on Canvas, 16 X 20

91. Alberta Field, Oil on Canvas, 16 X 20

92. Sunset Colours, Oil on Canvas, 16 X 20

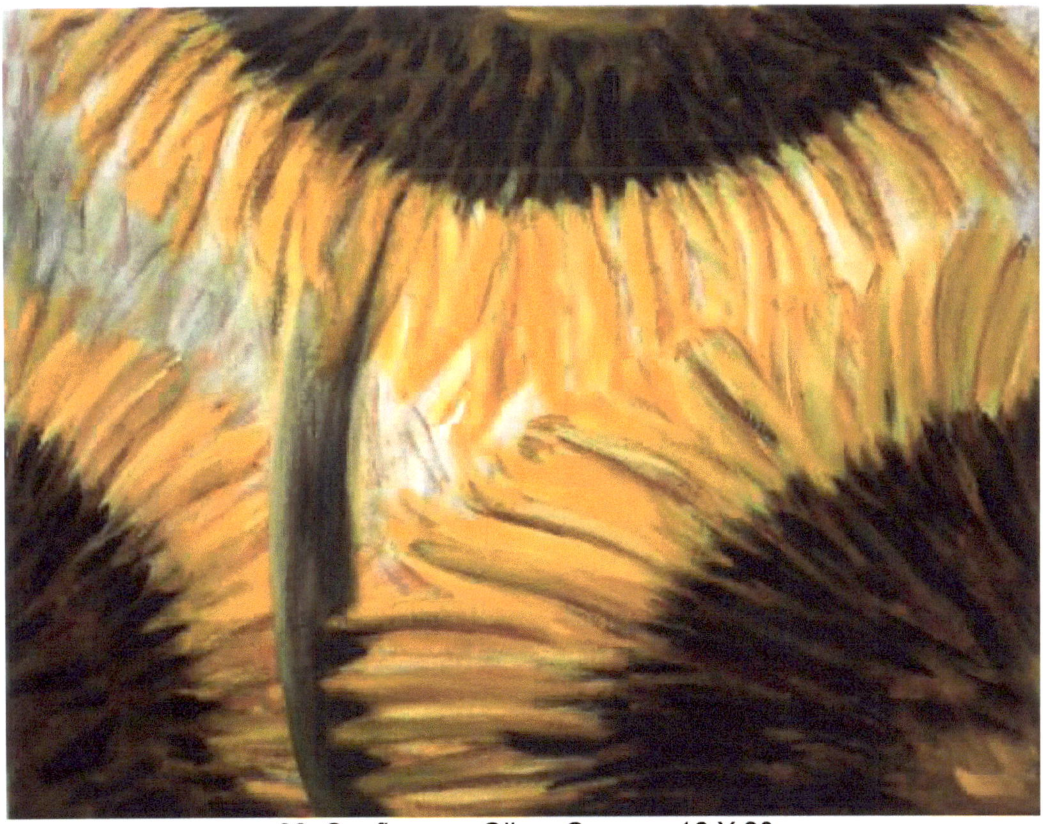

93. Sunflowers, Oil on Canvas, 16 X 20

94. Yosemite Field 3, Acrylic on Canvas, 16 X 20

95. Snow, Oil on Canvas, 28 X 22
(photo not found)

96. Fog, Oil on Canvas, 28 X 22
(based on photo # 165)

97. Tanning in Nice 2, Oil on Canvas, 20 X 16 (based on photo # 138)

98. Colours of a Creek, Oil on Canvas, 24 X 20 (based on photo # 168)

99. Alberta Rockies 1, Oil on Canvas, 18 X 24

100. Ducks' Manoeuvre at Lost Lagoon, Oil on Canvas, 11 X 14

101. Lucky Fence, Oil on Canvas, 11 X 14

102. **Crushing Waves** of Pacific Ocean, Oil on Acrylic on Canvas, 16 X 20

103. A River in Alberta, Oil on Canvas, 16 X 20

104. Lake in Whistler, BC, Oil on Canvas, 16 X 20

105. Dusk at Lost Lagoon 2, Oil on Canvas, 16 X 20

106. Juliet's *Original* Balcony!, Oil on Canvas, 20 X 16 (based on photo # 145)

107. Lions Gate Bridge, Oil on Acrylic on Canvas, 22 X 28

108. Yosemite Field 4, Oil on Canvas, 30 X 48 (based on photo # 71)

109. Lagoon at Whistler, Oil on Canvas, 20 X 24 (Based on Photo # 96)

110. Lost Lagoon 5, Oil on Canvas, 24 X 30 (based on photo # 46)

The Transition Dilemma

A mysterious urge at Howe Sound during a critical time in my life had instigated a decade of devotion to painting, as explained on page 21, but what had made me dump that seemingly sacred mission and switch to writing rather abruptly?

I recalled how this transition had felt urgent one day (as a parental duty) at the end of a long painting session mixed with doleful musing over my life, I cleaned the brushes and the plate —my faithful palette—and dropped my gloves on the painting table next to the plate. Not just the sight of the paint residue on the plate and gloves, but mainly the posture of the gloves tickled me, as if they were posing a philosophical (existential) question —NOW WHAT?—perhaps even like a clue from a divine or mysterious source to reassess my life even more seriously? I took a picture for fun.

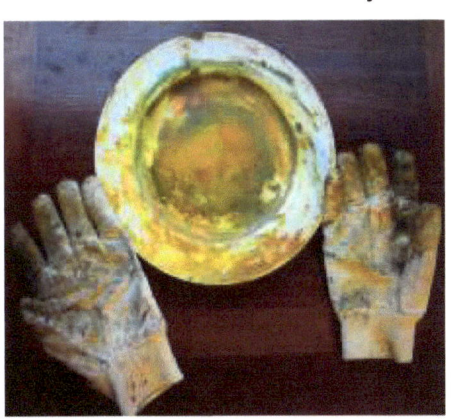

Now What?

Although the necessity of becoming a serious writer had felt smooth and natural after reassessing my life, it had also raised even my suspicions regarding my state of mind. After all, these passionate revelations, somewhat like getting tired of your lover overnight, feel worrisome to any sensible person. Nevertheless, this fast transition has sometimes felt like a huge mystery and dilemma of its own, especially because I had chosen hundred other pictures to paint. Putting aside that beautiful sketch I had prepared for a nude should have surely required a big switch in my head all by itself in line with new priorities, I reckon!

Luckily, I found a few plausible reasons for this radical transition eventually, too. For one thing, my sense of duty at the time to give my kids a realistic outlook of life in line with the growing global mayhem and the shoddy education they were getting at school and home had encouraged me to jot down my thoughts about socioeconomic issues to share with them somehow. More details about my worries about my kids' sense of reality are offered in Appendix A. Second, writing had felt necessary for releasing my frustrations regarding the damages we are inflicting upon Nature and ourselves so carelessly and irrationally merely out of greed and arrogance. Third, photographing and painting Nature for decades might have, ironically, made me more conscious of myself and life realities, instead of forgetting the whole world as my initial purpose of painting had been. All those forced seclusions and reflections, especially during the painting era, might have made me wonder and worry deeper about the looming catastrophes awaiting both nature and humans. Fourth, focusing on artistry might have felt silly as well under the circumstances. Fifth, my family's growing apathy had most likely also raised my stress and sufferings about humans' mentality, while I had hoped, *rather selfishly*, to lose myself in artistry. What are we trying to be or achieve as artists, families, or wise humans in our dying societies?

It seems likely that all these natural, philosophical, or mystical thoughts had forced me gauge my life purposes, delve into social issues, and tell real or fictional stories in line with my academic background and cynical mindset. This obsession for writing is now evident in this book as well, although I have tried to keep my stories short to leave more room for the painting pictures themselves! This book is supposed to be about them, not the painter, after all!—*especially one so unfaithful or unstable with regard to his urges for artistry!*

Nevertheless, the urgency of analysing and quoting our historical idiocies as vile, arrogant humans, including our choices of political, socioeconomic, and religious systems still supersede my passion for painting, although that period of my life feels a huge blessing of its own at a difficult time in my life. In fact, its delightful outcomes are my best pals these days when I walk around the house and stare at each painting a long time nostalgically.

Another big advantage of writing over painting is clearer to me now, too, in term of not requiring a physical possession of the final product. The task of looking after every painting, hanging it on a wall, or safeguarding it in a vault forever needs many devoted owners. Our writings also have a higher chance of surviving in the archives. These are good points that new artists should consider carefully before starting their careers, especially since justifying the purpose of art is becoming tough these days, anyway. Accordingly, the *Meaning and Value of Art* is elaborated further in the next section.

Ironically, my worries about my paintings' fate in a dying world—something that had instigated the idea of this book—also feel absurd especially, then! Still, I cannot stop wondering if *they will find new owners who'd appreciate them the way I have in the last two decades?* Do not our psyches operate so oddly and erratically too often?!

111. Around Mosquito Creek, Oil on Acrylic on Canvas, 20 X 16

112. Lush Green Field in BC, Oil on Canvas, 22 X 28

113. Feeding the Birds, Oil on Canvas, 20 X 16   114. Creek in Alberta, Oil on Canvas, 20 X 16

115. Winter in the Country, Acrylic on Canvas, 20 X 16

The Meaning and Value of Art

Good paintings have a magical power to enthral our spirits, as we stare at them for hours serenely. Then again, as noted before, it is getting harder every day to fathom the meaning and value of art while the world is falling apart and life's hardships are growing fast. Soon, we will be merely too occupied by social chaos, natural disasters, and personal sufferings to keep up with the burdens of living in our allegedly modern societies, let alone be artists. Nobody will have energy and time for pleasures, arts, or reflections, since we should struggle harder every day just to survive, repair ruins, manage our stress, and convince ourselves to keep living.

This very likely doomed outlook, which should be easily perceptible by humans, actually suggests that everything we achieve individually or collectively these days is futile until humans can establish a harmonious way of coexistence along with viable plans and commitments to elude their looming destiny. This means that at least 50%

of all people's interests and energies must be focused on humanity's long-term needs for survival during the next few centuries alongside our daily efforts to fit in and survive in society personally.

Art's goal and value for society should have been subject to its ultimate effect on humans' long-term welfare even before reaching this sad state of humanity, although we cannot blame primitive societies for lacking the knowledge and foresight that only modern humans have about their doomed future and still sticking to their obsolete mentalities and systems. In fact, the situation is getting too embarrassing when we all, including our artists, still pursue our ambitions and perceive art merely as a venue for social recognition, financial rewards, and personal need for achievement.

My thoughts and doubts about my own objectives around varied passions have been expressed in some parts of the book, especially on pages 89-91. Actually, most of my educations, occupations, and passions now feel worthless to the extent they have not played any significant role for addressing the sad state of humanity, though they have helped me forget the world and/or cope with life easier,

The following two precious quotes by Emile Zola and Sergei Rachmaninov about art seem relevant for the messages of this book as well.

<u>Emile Zola's Praise of Claude Monet</u>

*"Those painters who **love the times they live in** from the depth of their hearts and minds as artists perceive everyday realities in a different way. Above all, they try to penetrate the exact meaning of things."* From the book, Monet, A Retrospective, Edited by Charles F. Stuckey; Published by Hugh Lauter Levin Associates, 1985, page 38.

Emile's observation about some artists' need *to penetrate the exact meaning of things* is particularly succinct. Then again, it is simply too hard, nowadays, to **love the times we live in**, anyway! <u>Thus, it is hard to feel or be an artist, now!</u>

<u>A Quote about</u> Sergei Vasilievich Rachmaninov (1873-1943)

"I have chased three hares. Can I be certain that I have captured one?" Sergei is referring to his three passions as a composer, pianist, and conductor.

The answer to his question is clear in my opinion, as he stands on the eternal list of top 20-30 accomplished composers. His expertise as a pianist and conductor does not matter, anyway, due to their lack of longevity. *I am looking forward to telling him these facts in the heaven if he happens to be there.*

Sergei's comment also alarms me about chasing three hares myself, although more erratically, as mine have been somewhat unrelated passions. At least, Sergei's three hares had had the same genre and complementary purposes.

By the way, my father had encouraged me to study classical music and play piano at Tehran's music conservatory for two years until I stopped attending the school without telling my parents. Finally, the school expelled me, which led to my dad's dire reaction for over one year about my duplicity and pretensions. Yet, it was all my teacher's fault for being so demanding, but mostly for insulting and shaming his pupils regularly, especially a sensitive, pride soul like me!

Ironically, my parents did not ask my reason and I had not felt the need to tell them that I actually loved playing piano if my teacher would not bug me so much. Maybe they had thought that I did not like music, yet I had actually missed the chance of testing my talent and passion for music.

One less passion to confuse me, ha—all thanks to my silly teacher and assuming parents?!

Flirting with My Muse

My solemn acknowledgment about my muse's continued contributions to my writing passion had surely sounded naïve in the Author's Note at the beginning of the book. However, this holy belief has felt more plausible gradually during my long adventure in writing and turned into a deeper trust in a mystical power goading both my destiny and passions with both glorious and gloomy results. These rather spiritual convictions are actually elaborated in a few of my books systematically. Of course, my muse has been a nuisance often as well, especially for awakening me in the middle of the night sometimes to jot down her ideas immediately. Still, I have loved and trusted her in the journey we have been sharing through so much contemplation and writing. We seem to enjoy playing with each other like a kind of amusing, thoughtful flirtation.

Now, imagining my tireless efforts with so much passion for do this many paintings makes me believe that my muse had been responsible for, and instrumental in, that ten-year journey, too, before she had finally gotten tired and decided to focus on writing most likely for good reasons and higher priorities. These ideas sound childish, religious, or whatever, so it is useful to stress that surely I am not religious, if not a bigmouth atheist, as evident in my books. I believe in God, though, as an enigmatic creator of the universe, and possibly setting our fates, too, thru some unimaginable mechanisms. Then again, this belief has deepened my rational for denying all religious claims outright. *Surely, pampering some tender beliefs is vital for keeping our psyches and spirits high, too, to cope with escalating social deformations at least!*

117. Tree Rows, Acrylic on Canvas, 28X22   118. Shadowy Sidewalk, Acrylic on Canvas, 28X22

119 Seagulls at Stanley Park, Acrylic on Canvas, 20 X 16 (based on photo # 142)

120. Lost Lagoon 6, Acrylic on Canvas, 30 X 40 **(Sold)** (from photo # 45)

A Beginner's Paintings

Despite my enthusiasm to paint the serene scene of Howe Sound (front cover) that had prompted the idea of taking on painting, capturing that complex ambience had felt beyond my expertise for a year or so. Meanwhile, I read a book about painting techniques and began experimenting with simpler landscape subjects. Most of those initial works are shown below (#121-132) just for fun and to exhibit my initial artistry goaded by an immense despair at the time to rely on a challenging hobby in hopes of forgetting myself and the roots of my escalating tension. The humiliation that my new hobby had added to my burdens in the first few months had been both educational and funny, while my family had smirked at me and those initial paintings with pity. A broken, old man imitating a kindergartner had surely looked somewhat pathetic, yet I had persevered and learned humility! The dramatized story of my mindset and efforts during that bizarre period is offered wittily in my abstract novel, *My Lousy Life Stories,* in the chapters called *Howe Sound* and *The Villain in Vivian.*

My first painting, besides the *Woman in the White Dress,* which I had painted and given to Nick in 1980, is depicted below for fun! It is the **priceless** masterpiece my family had teased me about. Still, it shows my zeal from the start to paint the Lost Lagoon, as I had been drawn to that part of Stanley Park and taking hundreds of pictures of that busy sanctuary for many years already. The story about this first painting is also included in my abstract novel mentioned above. Mostly, though, this painting is useful for comparison with other paintings of the Lost Lagoon in this book, e.g. #120, to see how vastly one's expertise can improve in just a few years.

By the way, the idea of getting a painting instructor never appealed to me for many reasons, especially if I had to go to a class full of teenagers mocking me, too, like my family—an old man with big despair showing in his stealthy glances!

My initial paintings were done on acid free, archival papers, rather than canvas, as I could not imagine how serious this hobby might get. *Why many people paint on stones these day?—to save money, restore Stone Age customs, or as a novelty?!*

121. Lost Lagoon 7, Oil on Acid/Free Archival Paper, 9 X 12 (from photo # 45)

122. California Hills, Oil on Acid/Free Archival Paper, 12 X 16

123. Cherry Blossoms at Stanley Park 2, Oil on Acid/Free Archival Paper, 12 X 18 (based on photo #160)

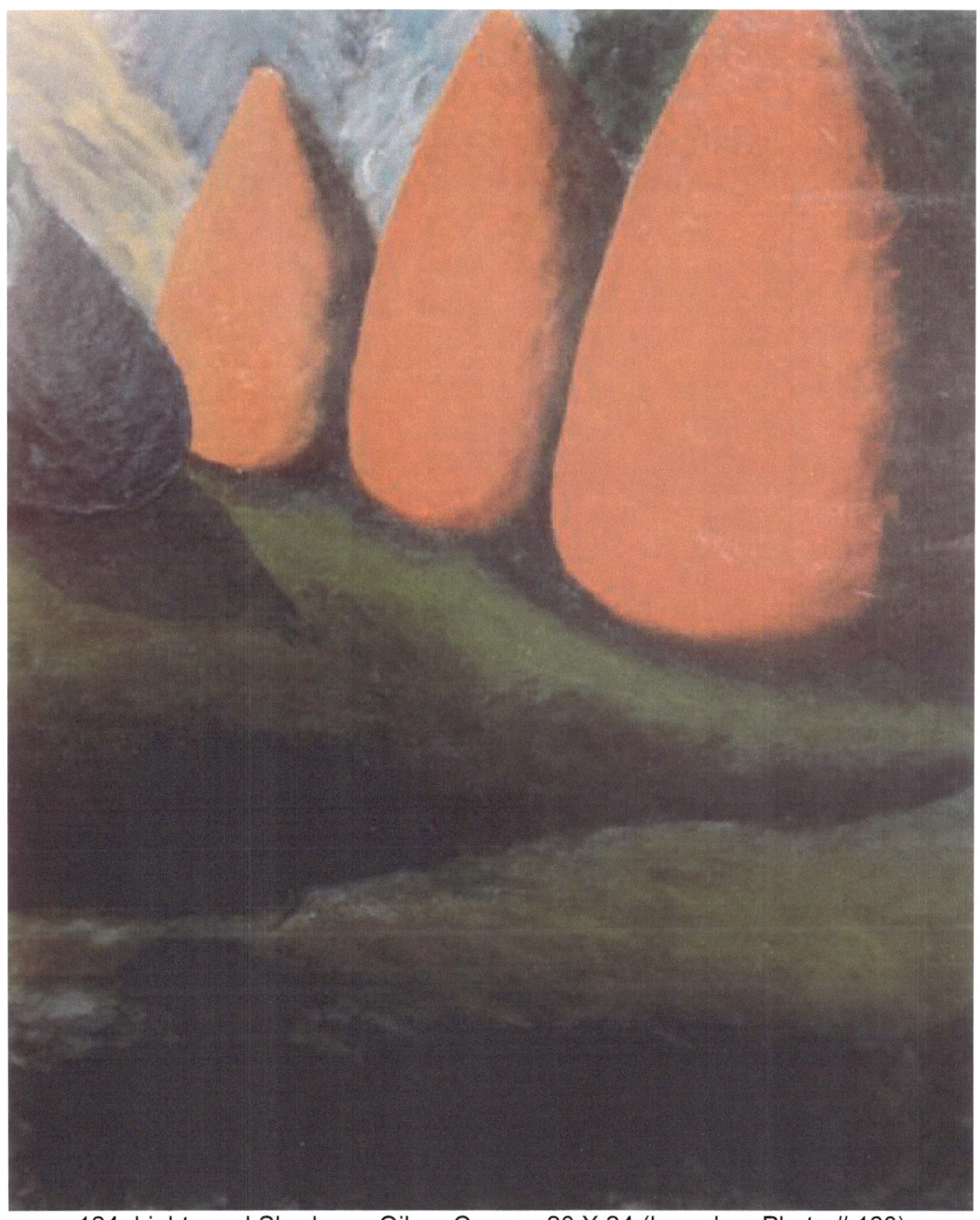
124. Lights and Shadows, Oil on Canvas 20 X 24 (based on Photo # 128)

Abstract Painting Popularity

After doing a dozen or so landscape paintings as a perturbed novice with mixed results and feelings, the idea of painting an abstract struck me with great hopes, the same way it probably entices all naïve beginners to bring the world to a standstill in awe like Picasso! Besides, perhaps I could become famous by being just an abstract painter, instead of struggling so anxiously to depict a romantic impression of Nature. Maybe I should just admit the difficulty of being a real painter with a mission to reveal the glory of Nature, which had been my goal of becoming a painter in the first place. Then again, I had the least expertise and sense about painting abstracts!

Thus, I asked the divine source that had put this darn idea of becoming an artist in my head, *'Please show me how to pour colours on canvas to make at least an abstract masterpiece without making a total fool of myself.'* My prayer was answered and the result, my first abstract painting, is shown on the next page. After staring at it a long time, trying to imagine something sensible about it, I felt tense and sad for not knowing what the heck it meant or represented. Yet, as another of my eccentricities perhaps, it felt crucial to know what I had tried to say or if it was at least a beautiful drawing. My tortured spirit fretted and screamed, *'Be honest with yourself at least!'*

At last, I imagined the painting could possibly represent a fish, turtle, bird, snake, or whale if I just added an eye. Then again, the idea of imposing an eye after the fact, beyond the original idea in my head,—just to make it look sensible—felt particularly bizarre and unconventional in itself, for an abstract painting. It also felt like cheating! Facing a big dilemma for a few days, at last I decided to add the damn eye and move on! I had tortured myself long enough! **'You must always know what you are doing with a goal from the start,'** is a principle I love to follow as much as possible!

Still, this whole exercise during my first abstract artistry made me ponder some philosophical or psychological questions as well, *as usual*. In particular, I wondered what force, intuition, or goal really makes many of us modern humans proceed to paint something that we do not know its meaning or purpose. We usually have no initial perception of the task, nor are even keen to ponder what we have imagined, done, or tried to accomplish. Do we do it just for the heck of it by random mixing of lines and colours, because we have no patience or talent to do a real painting? Can anything be considered art, even if it looks pretty, when it has no special message or meaning? Are we merely trying to be innovative regardless of its likely intention and technical values? *Have we modern humans been treating all aspect of our existence, even art and music, only superficially?*

Still, I have painted a half dozen abstracts, while striving to find some kind of meaning for each along with a logical name. At the same time, I love semi-abstract style that often exerts a message and contains technical complexity. In that context, I like *I Scream 2*, #63 on page 48, in particular. Its succinct message alone is heartfelt for me at least. I hope the name of the painting, especially # 2, is elucidating as well, *although I do not like to explain everything always!*

Anyway, a likely, rather obvious, reason for the prevalence of abstract paintings crossed my mind later considering how faster my few abstract paintings had been completed compared with my regular and semi-abstract paintings. Accordingly, the popularity of painting in pure abstract, nowadays, seems to confirm humans' rising laziness and impatience even for artistry, while also losing their knack for meanings and clear messages to share and enrich humanity or prevent its doom at least. Our obsessions for novelty, individualism, and similar naive ideologies are manifesting in our artistic expressions as well, and they are destroying the essence of societies and humanity. Accordingly, it is also getting harder to grasp our needs as individuals or a species. We simply do not find enough sense or incentive to stress on humanity even in such a trying time when socioeconomic and political systems around the globe are collapsing so hastily. Instead, our systematic denial of rooted problems and our lousy remedies reveal the enormity of social and personal numbness. Ironically, these vile human tendencies are all bizarre symptoms of modernism apparently. They are now manifesting even in our foolish idealism to be innovative and artistic just for flaunting our ingenuity! Meanwhile, my relentless cynicism and whining make even me ask myself, *'Is there anything that you do not criticize readily so harshly?'*

Luckily, though, I always realize fast that none of these social follies is my fault!

125. A Fish, Turtle, Bird, Snake, or Whale, Oil on Acid/Free Archival Paper, 11 X 16

126. Endless Crash at Pacific Ocean, Oil on Acid/Free Archival Paper, 9 X 12

127. An Orderly Flight at Sunset, Oil on Archival Paper, 9 X 12 (from photo # 120)

128. Alberta Rockies 3, Oil on Acid/Free Archival Paper, 11 X 14 (from Photo # 155)

129. Waterfall, Oil on Acid/Free Archival Paper, 12 X 9

130. A Tiny Creek in Whistler, (same as 124, Oil...)

131. Sunset at West Vancouver, Oil on Paper, 12 X 18

132. Alberta Rockies 2, Oil on Paper, 9 X 12

All along, trying to find viable meanings for my paintings in various styles, especially abstracts, had been a challenge, too, though impressionism and realism had felt most viable for interpreting nature's grandeur. Semi-abstracts, especially painting #63, had been inspired by big emotional messages, too, besides the curiosity initiating every painting. Meanwhile, all these artistic curiosities mixed with a deep urge for a practical life purpose have probably been satiated at the risk of losing common life's pleasure that others pretend to enjoy. *At least my dire curiosity has not killed me yet, although it has felt more acute and worrisome than what any prying cat might be accused of!*

A Reconstructed Painting

When my dear father passed away and I went to Iran for related affairs, I found a large, damaged painting (#133) in his suite. It raised my curiosity about the painter and the chance of restoring it. The rotting canvas was taken off its broken frame and shipped to Vancouver upon my return, while wondering why the painter had used such a thin canvas and a narrow, frail frame for this big painting. Years later, I put a new layer of thick canvas behind the original one that was worn and torn in small places and the paint had peeled off in some areas, and then re-stretched it on a solid frame. The white spots in the painting show the main damaged areas.

Wondering who the painter had been, the slight, but plausible, chance that my father had painted it himself could not be dismissed outright. He had been a curious, multi-talented person, appreciated art and music, had a large collection of classical recordings, and went to symphonic performances in Tehran and Los Angeles during the years he had lived in Los Angeles. He was a relatively good violinist and played in a community orchestra during annual celebrations. He was a great photographer with the love of nature, as I mentioned before, and he spent lots of time gardening, too. I found a large amount of his writings in Persian as well, which I brought back with me to Vancouver and read nostalgically.

Sadly, though, his writings mostly revealed his mental decline after a long coma in an ICU in Los Angeles. His rather radical claims in his writings about mysticism after his Near Death Experience during the coma felt farfetched, while he had turned into a devote spiritualist or modern Muslim swiftly after a lifetime of womanizing and sinful existence. His wild mentality and lifestyle had probably also led to divorcing my mother after thirty years of marriage, the same way I have managed my life. *In all, it seems we had inherited the same peculiar genes largely!!*

Anyway, I could not just ignore the slight likelihood of my dad's urge to test his knack for painting, too, just for the heck of it or out of boredom. Thus, I decided at last to either reconstruct or discard this painting that was taking so much space with no value without a fundamental repair. I realized my inability to restore the original image even if I grasped the painter's intention and ignored a few technical issues with the branches' designs. At last, redoing the painting without losing its main design, had felt like a good compromise in line with my patience and taste. Especially, showing my personal sense of that scene had felt fair compared with the options of either keeping that rather pale and torn canvas or throwing it away ruthlessly. After all, inserting the kind of mood appealing to me seemed imperative if I were going to spend time to do an acceptable job.

At the end, I took the risk, apologized to the painter, and began throwing paint on the canvas. The original and reconstructed images are shown in the next page. Still, I am a bit sorry for changing the painting's original mood by making it darker in line with my depressing mood seeking a ray of light. I have always meant, of course, to work some more on it and improve it based on some new impressions and colour changes in my head. All I need is some time and energy! At least its basic format remains intact in the midst of new heavenly sunrays of hope that I have added for soothing my psyche in the dark world we live. *I'll make it lovelier soon, dad, I promise!* **I hope so!!**

133. A Forest Mood, Oil on Canvas, 50 X 75 (Before Reconstruction)

133. A Forest Mood, Oil on Canvas, 50 X 75 (After Reconstruction)

Behind the Scene (Part Two)

Besides the objective of archiving my paintings, giving myself another opportunity to reassess my life choices along with my peculiar dilemmas and quirks had been a big motive for preparing this book, *just in case there was still time to change my lifestyle!* Especially, recalling the story behind each painting nostalgically when photographing them had helped me confirm that honouring my passions within a rather secluded, disciplined lifestyle had been a right choice for me, *overall*, although maintaining this balance has been hard and stressful, especially in the absence of a loyal family.

Still, only if you like psychological and philosophical conjectures keep reading this section, as it merely offers a crude perspective of our curious psyches behind the scene, which stirs both our artistic or scholarly interests as well—for better or worse, although we often cannot say which, not even in our final years. In my case, spending so many years on varied fields of education, painting, and writing about irresolvable socioeconomic/political problems often appears pointless in the big scheme of things when the world seems incapable of eluding its frightful fate, and existence is feeling sadder and vaguer every day. Still, I try to console myself that research, painting, and writing have at least kept me rather amused in a healthier way than what majority do for survival and curbing social pains. *Then again, ironically, even my intention here to explain my spiritual and philosophical grasp of a likely truth behind my life choices and mentality sounds pathetic, as if I am trying to justify my existence to you and myself!*

On the one hand, getting philosophical in a picture book is bizarre, in addition to exposing my eccentric mindset after enduring a long, precarious existence around academic, artistic, and humanitarian urges. On the other hand, even some images of nature incite our psyches to wander curiously thru philosophical reflections and get idealistic or spiritual. Accordingly, adding some hints about my mushy emotions and dilemmas along with the paintings' backgrounds had felt sincere in showing varied baffling forces *behind the scene* stirring our psyches and personalities in line with our curiosities. Despite the common motto about free will and our efforts to stay rational with our life choices, some mystical powers seem to conspire with our peculiar genes to make us choose certain life paths possibly mixed with artistic or altruistic urges. Accordingly, building and embracing a personal life philosophy helps us think more practically, relax a little, form our faiths better, and respect nature more authentically for both its endless glamour and harsh ecological impacts. These simple sentiments and beliefs have helped me analyse, and sometime even cherish, my life choices, in spite of their likely risks or questionable outcomes. *Gosh, these touchy confessions might now entice so many beautiful women rush to relieve my loneliness!!!*

Beauty and love feel precious and urgent as well, except that their powers and values shrink in the absence of meaning or essence, or if egoism and naiveté hinder our abilities to grasp love and beauty sincerely. Thus, they have also turned into big hurdles and dilemmas for modern humans. Love, particularly, feels meaningless and it hurts when compassion is lacking—a gloomy reality that is deepening in today's lifestyles, while family relationships and humanity are falling apart so hastily.

Surely, life choices have become less justifiable and reliable as we have tried to be modern and happy. After all, our ambitions, even academic and artistic ones, demand lots of sacrifice and flexibility to endure so many risks and family (public) retorts, especially if we like to boost our authenticities and identities, too. Then again, our passions, e.g., painting landscapes to revere nature, writing about society to express our frustrations, or exploring the essence of existence to fathom the depth of humans' ignorance often jeopardize our views of life/social realities, including family and social obligations. The crude sense of individualism we try to parade so naively feels shaky, too, even in our heads, as we try to develop our convictions for building and managing our personalities. Especially, we get confused about the life path we have chosen either consciously or by the force of our whims and egos. Harmonizing these conflicting existential challenges along with common and urgent life priorities turns into a big, messy mission by itself and takes a big toll of our mental energies.

Ironically, even humans' precious traits, such as curiosity, love, and principles often clash and turn into dire nuisances for keeping our mental balance and a stable personality. This happens, for example, when discipline (to honour our beliefs and principles) makes us hesitant in terms of testing our curiosities or when our curiosities override our sense of discipline, especially if they make us forget our authentic or urgent needs, fall in love naively, dream habitually, or live just for today.

Normally, clinging to the mainstream lifestyle mixed with our *supposedly* sensible beliefs, visions, and ambitions gets priority for pragmatists, while we seek the wisdom and discipline required for physical and mental health in a rather stable life path. Still, our passions and curiosities, zeal for a meaningful existence, erratic emotional needs, and mental insecurities often dull our senses of pragmatism and reality.

Meanwhile, many conflicting forces in the universe and society also ambush our psyches constantly, especially at some particular life junctions and moments of reflections. We try to coordinate them in hopes of an easier existence with lesser confusion, yet these conflicting urges, forces, and realities distort our outlooks and health. In the end, facing so many dilemmas just to fulfil our daily needs remains a lifetime challenge even for those of us who do not crave social popularity or acceptance and those who have lost touch with reality already due to their wide ranges of personal insecurities and whims. Handling these lingering confusions in our tired psyches becomes merely a matter of personal wisdom and character.

Personally, letting my curiosities and muse influence my destiny rather erratically through different passions, despite my zeal to stay practical and authentic, has not been easy on my psyche. Then again, the process has felt natural and inevitable for fostering my identity and mental health in a simple life, while also hoping to know the meanings and goals of my actions and passions regularly. The succinct comments by Emil Zola and Sergei Rachmaninov quoted on page 78 appear to support my mixed sentiments noted on these pages, too.

Naturally, the task of curbing my curiosities and urges to force a logical balance among my life options vs. dilemmas has felt both painful and precious, but possibly ordained for pursuing a self-fulfilling life around a few passions in line with some deep beliefs and principles. The sudden urge 25 years ago pushing me to begin painting many tableaux has felt fruitful as a timely hobby (or perhaps even a divine distraction) during a hectic period of my life, like a sacred tool for meditation, although writing has proven even more potent in keeping my psyche intact. In the end, the amount of time, patience, and efforts I have devoted to reflection thru art, while keeping a demanding job in government and fighting with a sinister family, feels surreal to me, as it mostly shows how hard we try, often in vain, to distract our minds and elude our gloomy lives and social realities that are getting harsher every year to bear or at least understand.

Fortunately, nature has remained a common denominator in all my passions and helped my psyche reconcile my life choices, principles, and ambitions in search of meaningful life purposes and peace. Nature has regulated both my inspirations and reflections regularly somehow, even for my academic research, like a sacred force keeping me energetic and hopeful in a baseless society. These beliefs also appear to make even the hassles of extra work and mental challenges feel more natural and bearable to some of us than relying on alcohol, drugs, and constant socializing to face or define our boring beings. Most importantly, my paintings of nature around me have boosted my energy and joy all along, like many faithful, pleasant children I had craved and missed a lifetime foolishly in my real ones!

Surely, keeping such an optimistic mindset is not easy, since even our passions often heighten our dilemmas about existence when the value and meaning of our creations also feel more doubtful daily in the skim of things with humanity most likely reaching its end soon. Actually, this dark reality questions the value of most human efforts these days, including professional sports, cultural and historical efforts, space explorations, etc. Meanwhile, these escalating dilemmas show how oddly our brains must now work constantly under such an immense level of psychological pressures! Even choosing the means of conveying our feelings through art, words, compassion, love, or theories becomes baffling and personal, in particular if one tries to mix all these mediums in one's mind or a book like this!

Ironically, in the end, it is hard to say if one has been lucky or failed terribly in defining a meaningful path of life for oneself due to one's rather conflicting urges for experimentations and discipline! Not knowing which one is another dilemma, although I feel content more often than rueful, just because I believe the alternative would have been much more painful and disastrous. Then, having 134 paintings to support my sentiments and words in this book feels like the icing on a tiny apple pie. Gauging the outcomes of my artistic efforts and thoughts in this book has been fun, too, while they have possibly also saved at least 134,000 additional words of wisdom that I would have been inclined to include in this book to express my views of life's mysteries confusing most of us. A book about my photographs would soon follow as well.

By the way, despite my views all along about the looming doomsday, ironically, I still remain concerned about the destiny of the 134 paintings I have kept around me rather selfishly as my only soulful companions and creations these days. Sometimes, they appear to be mourning their fates around a pensive, possessive spirit, too, and then possibly in the hands of some strangers after my departure! In this case, in fact, every one of them is really saying a thousand words to me regularly, while I both enjoy staring at them and grieve their most likely sad fate similar to mine. Simply, the chances that they end up in the right hands remain as doubtful and gloomy as my chance of finding a fantastic, loyal companion has felt last ten years.

Nonetheless, both fussing over my paintings' fate and getting attached to them more every day, while missing the dozen or so that were sold prematurely, have been rather frustrating as well. In fact, I pay three times or more for my sold paintings if their current owners are willing to depart with them. At the same time, the oddity of my mushy attachment to these paintings feels pathetic and silly, *sometimes,* although I often develop similar level of attachment to all soulful or inspiring objects, including some special plants that I regularly grow from scratch and they turn into big, beautiful trees, mostly outdoors, in the exotic shapes I try to mould them.

Now, I wonder if my current writing addiction would also bear the same destiny as my passions for photography and painting have endured when the futility of my efforts to address humanity sinks in my dull head deeper at last and I accept that nothing—no words, philosophy, hostilities, wars, religions, compassion, logic, faiths, science, images of beautiful Nature, love, natural disasters, or anything else we have concocted so far to boost humanity—would have the power to overcome humans' greedy urges and demented mentality, not even for the sake of their survival.

Finally, only if you are wealthy and serious about investing your money in the masterpieces exhibited in this book check out Appendix B on the last page for some invaluable insight. It offers a very conservative suggested price for the first 38 listed paintings at the beginning of the book, plus my two favourites—merely for offering a general idea when all the paintings are sold only after my departure and the proceeds wired to my varied saving accounts in the heaven!

Otherwise, just close the book properly for taking another good look at my self-portrait on the back cover! *Doesn't he look puzzled behind that cocky smirk?*

****

Mentioning the amazing investment opportunities in Appendix B after my departure to the heaven makes me wonder about the kind of socioeconomic/political systems that might guide humans over there without annoying God too much there as well! What kind of society might keep humans calm and united there and why cannot we even imagine a simple replica of that system to live more peacefully now. Surely, capitalism and other foolish ideologies we have invented here so proudly, such as democracy, human rights, and freedom of speech, would not work and surely not allowed in the heaven! Is even the concept of society or marriage relevant over there at all? Is God or His son(s) ruling rather autocratically out of necessity? *How many sons does God have whom he'd decided to spare from us?* Are not we going to be bored to our teeth without greed, rivalry, ambitions, sex, and art filling our days? Would we be allowed to socialize and what kind of language we would be using to communicate rationally and peacefully for eternity. Is God going to grant us a tame nature upon entering the heaven, so that we can get along fine? If yes, why did not He do it from the start?

Maybe these are the sort of issues that God is still trying to sort out before deciding on the judgment day and opening the heaven's door to a few *allegedly best creatures*. Surely, He already knows that even the best of us are unable to get along peacefully even a day, never mind eternally, while we would be spoiled quickly if He gives us all kinds of privileges that we imagine will be available to us in the heaven, while we walk around proudly for being selected as His favourites. Thus, for now, most likely the heaven remains empty in vain until He can possibly figure out a way for keeping human brains manageable, and after all final preparations for our arrival are safely complete! *I can hardly wait… The last painting, next page, actually shows my vision of that journey.*

Sorry, dear readers… Sadly, some heretical questions often revolve in my silly head! Now, it seems that finding any excuse to include some blasphemy in my books has become an addiction, although for an allegedly sacred purpose, besides humour: To make us all also think somewhat more realistically and consistently about so many ideas and stories that naïve humans have invented throughout their dull, destructive history to entertain themselves and keep some hope about the value of existence. But, really, if any truth has ever existed behind prevalent religious claims, why have not still these fanatical clergies provided any plausible answers to the basic questions raised in the last two paragraphs, so that humans can possibly fathom a more viable socioeconomic and political structure to avoid so much chaos and pains?

'God forgive your idiocy,' my dear religious grandma yelled at me often anytime I teased her with similar heresies during my adolescence. You, dear readers, forgive me, too! Only God knows what exactly goes on in my foolish head **behind the scene**!

*****

The painting in the next page is about me as an old man on the path to heaven in line with the tale of a gloomy painter called Darren Durant in my *Persian Moons* novel.

<u>An atheist being so certain about going to heaven deserves a monumental prize!</u> Can you see at least three devilish, divine, and innocent faces in the clouds confusing me on my way to the heaven? These 3 ghostly images in the clouds also restate the 3 symbolic figures in painting #63, *I Scream 2!*

134. Path to Heaven, Oil on Canvas, 40 X 30

Appendix A
A Major Reason for Transition from Painting to Writing

As noted in the Author's Note, a major reason for switching from painting to writing related to my immense sense of parental duty, while I had been jotting down my concerns and thoughts for years about family relationships and the way the youths are educated (misled) in societies. Then, I began organizing those ideas in the trilogy, *Doubts and Decisions for Living*, which was published in 2014. A quote from that trilogy, volume I, pages 3-4, shows my sentiments then and even more so now after all the subsequent changes in my relationship with my family.

"… Telling the story of my family's immigration to Canada has been only for stressing the agony that most parents willingly bear for their kids. Yet, as my children got older, it seemed that I had an even more taxing task ahead. I felt that my main responsibility as a parent was to answer their questions and guide them during adolescence when all kids face the highest amount of doubts about themselves and life and must make very serious decisions in a short span of time. As a parent, my duty to enlighten them, if I could, appeared ten times more important and difficult than all the hardships of bringing them to Canada and providing them with a comfortable life. Preparing my kids for the hassles of living even in modern societies with inefficient economies, volatile job markets, phony lifestyles, and materialistic values, felt crucial, while hoping to teach them think rather independently, instead of getting addicted to so much vanity blindly. I had to tell them what life was all about—if I could. Did I understood life myself and did my kids cared about hearing my interpretation of life? The answer to both questions seemed to be a resounding 'no.' I did not know much about life myself, and my children, like all other kids, were not interested in listening to the advice of their old-fashioned parents. Still, it felt imperative to me to pursue my mission somehow. I had to establish my opinions about the main features of human life and struggles for my own benefit at least. Maybe I could then share my plausible conclusions with others, too, especially youths who strive to build themselves and their futures in such confusing societies. Then, it dawned on me that it would be more productive to write a book gradually and systematically, instead of offering random ideas here and there. Then, maybe my kids and others would take the trouble of reading this account of a concerned parent's wisdom leisurely on their own!"

I started the above noted trilogy fifteen years ago and finished it in three years thru extensive research and contemplation, yet I failed to draw my kids' interests to read it carefully. The reasons for my failure are explained in the Epilogue of Volume I of *Doubts and Decisions for Living*. Apparently, we all prefer to discover our naiveties about existence and societies the hard way—after so many years of struggling and stress perhaps—, if at all.

At the same time, it is astonishing how we, especially our conceited leaders, believe and act as if nothing is too fundamentally wrong with humanity, educational systems, religions, socioeconomic systems, social ideologies, and our personalities, and that we are not heading for doomsday expeditiously. All this negligence is just baffling, especially considering humans' spiritual curiosity and spirits to explore their beings. Ironically, while our genes and society suffocate our fundamental urge for decency, some of us can still learn to redeem our spirits and find peace.

Appendix B
A Conservative Suggested Price List for Paintings after My Departure

A very conservative, well-construed price list is suggested below only for the first 38 paintings shown in the List of Paintings, plus #63 and #134 (my favourites). This basic price range applies to the rest of the paintings, though, based on their varied merits. Let us hope we can at least trust the next generation with this simple chore![†]

Painting # Name	Medium	Size (inches)	Price (US$)
1. Howe Sound	Acrylic on Canvas	20 X 24	23,698,952
2. Self-portrait 2006	Oil on Canvas	24 X 20	66,606,777
3. Yosemite Tree I	Oil on Canvas	40 X 30	48,558,904
4. Mosquito Creek 1	Oil on Canvas	28 X 22	6,798,430
5. Mosquito Creek 2	Oil on Canvas	28 X 22	4,969,000
6. A View of Howe Sound	Oil on Canvas	36 X 48	8,088,251
7. Lost Lagoon 4	Oil on Canvas	36 X 48	3,105,481
8. Lost Lagoon Set, 1	Oil on Canvas	48 X 36	6,116,573
9. Lost Lagoon Set, 2	Oil on Canvas	48 X 36	6,116,573
10. Lost Lagoon Set, 3	Oil on Canvas	48 X 36	6,116,573
11. Life's Oddities	Acrylic on Canvas	24 X 24	1,742,222
12. San Francisco Hills at Dusk	Oil on Canvas	30 X 40	2,989,780
13. Poppy Field	Oil on Canvas	36 X 54	4,186,019
14. Stanley Park Hills	Oil on Canvas	36 X 18	1,059,897
15. Lonesome Tree II	Oil on Canvas	36 X 18	1,329,000
16. Mosquito Creek 3 (MC)	Acrylic on Canvas	24 X 20	2,199,999
17. Secret Path at Mosquito Creek	Oil on Canvas	40 X 30	20,335,420
18. Water Lilies 1	Oil on Canvas	30 X 24	14,023,230
19. Water Lilies 2	Oil on Canvas	30 X 24	3,735,003
20. Edmonton Park 1	Oil on Canvas	40 X 30	1,546,823
21. Water Lilies 3	Oil on Canvas	48 X 36	1,924,995
22. Tanning in Nice 1	Oil on Canvas	40 X 30	966,787
23. Edmonton Park 2	Oil on Canvas	18 X 24	1,546,993
24. Dusk Mood in a Wide Field	Acrylic on Canvas	16 X 20	2,999,012
25. Yosemite Tree II	Oil on Canvas	28 X 22	11,430,430
26. Kenmore Creek	Acrylic on Canvas	28 X 22	11,765,430
27. Mosquito Creek 4	Oil on Canvas	24 X 20	11,767,228
28. Pacific Ocean from Whytecliff Park	Acrylic on Canvas	21½ X 35½	1,511.232
29. Silhouette	Oil on Canvas	36 X 24	2,699,773
30. Spring in Mountains	Oil on Canvas	30 X 40	1,035,098
31. Yosemite Field II	Oil on Canvas	24 X 30	1,038,198
32. A Cozy Corner at the Gallery	Oil on Canvas	30 X 24	8,297,528
33. Sneaky Tulip	Oil on Acrylic on Canvas	14 X 11	286,498
34. Alberta Park 1	Oil on Canvas	28 X 22	475,916
35. Banff, Alberta 1	Oil on Canvas	48 X 38	4,738,455
36. Banff, Alberta 2	Oil on Canvas	43 X 38	4,938,905
37. Jean Pierre's Living Room	Acrylic on Canvas	24 X 18	6,406,103
38. My Dinning Room	Acrylic on Canvas	22 X 28	7,441,934
63. I Scream 2	**Oil on Canvas**	**22 X 28**	**118,954,870**
134. Path to Heaven	Oil on Canvas	40 X 30	76,038,455

[†] **Of course, I might have over or under priced some paintings due to my special feelings, or experts' comments, about them, but overall the prices sound very fair to me. Enjoy!**

www.ingramcontent.com/pod-product-compliance
Lightning Source LLC
Chambersburg PA
CBHW042013150426
43196CB00002B/26